GOOD SPIRITUAL HYGIENE

A.J. Lykosh & Bob Perry

MAKARIOS
PRESS

Esmont, VA

Makarios Press
P.O. Box 28, Esmont, VA 22937

© 2022 by A.J. Lykosh & Bob Perry

All rights reserved. No part of this book may be reproduced in any form except in the case of brief quotations without written permission from Makarios Press.

Scripture in NIV unless otherwise stated.

Design: Nate Braxton

ISBN 978-1-956561-34-0

Printed in the United States of America

CONTENTS

Introduction 7

Protection
The Biblical Prayer of Protection 15
The Practical Prayer of Protection 19
The Prayer of Protection 21
Our Responsibility 23
Next-level Protection... 27
Strong WarfarePrayer 29
Always Pray andDon't Give Up.................................... 31

Cleansing
After Every Interaction 39
The Cutting-Free Prayer 41
For the Empathetic Among Us 43
Prayer for aBurden Bearer 47
The Prayer fora Fresh Start 49

Conclusion
Blessing... 53

Appendix
Appendix A 59
Appendix B 63

INTRODUCTION

Our bodies naturally produce waste products: we exhale, we sweat, we eliminate.

We also wash our hands and brush our teeth and bathe.

We don't think, "Wow, how distressing that I need to shower! Why is my body dirty again already?"

Rather, we recognize that elimination is part of the natural process of living, and we take the few minutes to get clean, and then go about our day.

In our homes, too, we take out the trash when the receptacle fills.

We don't then go pick through the trash ... we dispose of it quickly, and we move on with life.

The focus of the day is not the trash. The focus is life. We practice good hygiene because we are alive.

But even as a house gets stinky very quickly if the trash isn't emptied, and even as a body dies very quickly if it can't eliminate, so it is in the spiritual realm, as well.

We talk to someone, and sometimes the conversation gets us down.

We live in a world with decay and death, and at times we find ourselves sad.

This sadness isn't wrong.

Or, rather, it's no more wrong than the need to take a

shower after sweating on a hike, or the need to brush our teeth after a meal.

We shower and brush because we're alive and life is good, and we need to clean up because we've been living.

Similarly, we need to pray because God gives us relationships and work and ministries, and we need to clean up because we've been living.

Not a problem. Just a reality.

This booklet teaches how to practice good spiritual hygiene, prayers that can help keep you feeling refreshed.

These prayers aren't meant to be the focus of a day. They're more like taking out the trash. Pray them, perhaps once a day, and then move on.

In this booklet, we focus on two directions: protection, and cutting free.

The late healing prayer minister and teacher Francis MacNutt recommended the prayer of protection before a time of prayer ministry, and the cutting-free prayer after.

These two directions in prayer serve two different functions.

Think of one as the shower and deodorant and the beginning of the day, getting ready.

And the other as like the shower after a good workout, cleaning up.

Practically, though, in my life, everything runs a bit together, so we usually pray the prayer of protection and the cutting-free prayer back-to-back every morning.

These prayers have transformed our prayer life.

Begin to include these prayers in your daily life, and you will notice a tremendous, shocking difference.

That said: we each get to be on our journey. If any of these prayers don't feel right to you—don't pray them!

My friend Cindy McFaden recommended to me, during a rough season, Dr. Cindy Trimm's "Atomic Power of Prayer," an hour-long warfare prayer, available online.

I listened for about ten seconds before I felt agitated.

When I confessed this, rather shamefacedly, Cindy McFaden said, "Honesty is freedom."

Which I took to mean: not all prayers are for all people at all times and in all circumstances.

If a prayer feels off to you, there are two possible reasons:

1. It's not a prayer for you in this season, and the Lord is pushing back to say, "Don't pray this one."
2. It is a prayer for you in this season, and the enemy is pushing back to say, "Don't pray this one."

The only way to know is to ask God: *Is this prayer for me right now?*

And see what he says!

— Bob & AJ

PROTECTION

THE BIBLICAL PRAYER OF PROTECTION

Finally, be strong in the Lord and in his mighty power. Put on the full armor of God, so that you can take your stand against the devil's schemes. For our struggle is not against flesh and blood, but against the rulers, against the authorities, against the powers of this dark world and against the spiritual forces of evil in the heavenly realms.[1]

My college mentor Connie Anderson, now head of Intercessory Prayer for the college ministry InterVarsity, told of an interaction with a seasoned overseas missionary.

———•❋•———

"You need to daily pray protection over yourself and your family."

I put that in a category in my head named, "Things I should do, but don't, and feel rather guilty about."

My husband and I have always had an apostolic gifting to plant, or encourage those who are planting, new works of God in areas with little witness. Soon the opposition of the enemy became nearly unbearable.

We began to take our missionary's advice seriously, and started to pray together daily with a commitment to protect ourselves in prayer from the enemy.

Peter describes the evil one: "Be alert and of sober mind. Your enemy the devil prowls around like a roaring lion *looking for someone to devour.*"[2]

Do you ever feel like you are being devoured? Or maybe you have a loved one struggling?

How can you make this stop?

Paul gives some familiar instructions.

Finally, be strong in the Lord and in his mighty power. Put on the full armor of God, so that you can take your stand against the devil's schemes. For our struggle is not against flesh and blood, but against the rulers, against the authorities, against the powers of this dark world and against the spiritual forces of evil in the heavenly realms. Therefore put on the full armor of God, so that when the day of evil comes, you may be able to stand your ground, and after you have done everything, to stand. Stand firm then, with the belt of truth buckled around your waist, with the breastplate of righteousness in place, and with your feet fitted with the readiness that comes from the gospel of peace. In addition to all this, take up the shield of faith, with which you can extinguish all the flaming arrows of the evil one. Take the helmet of salvation and <u>the sword of the Spirit, which is the word of God.</u>[3]

To illustrate this idea, Vic Black tells a story of a vision where he popped his head up in the middle of a field. On one side were all the horrible demons, and on the other side were the angelic heavenly host.

And there was his head poking up in the middle of the field.

Then God the Father caught his eye. And God looked at Vic with love, but maybe a bit of concern, too, and said, Where is your armor?!

And the vision is a bit humorous. You can imagine it playing out like a cartoon: orcs and goblins on one side, gorgeous holy warriors on the other side.

And in the middle, a man clad in long-johns.

Oops!

Why would anyone go into battle without armor?

We are in a battle! So let's put on our armor.

Which all sounds well and good. But what does it look like, practically?

The late Francis MacNutt said of prayer, "Everyone gets to play."

Husbands and wives together, a single parent alone, college students ... everyone gets to play.

For Connie, she and her husband kneel at the couch each morning. Together, they ask the Lord for protection this day. Her husband lines up the family members in his head, and as he prays, he imagines dressing each one of them in the piece of armor as he prays it out loud. It's fine if the picture is blurry or not perfectly clear. That's normal, especially at first.

Lord, I put on the breastplate of righteousness, the belt of truth, the shoes fitted with the preparation of the gospel of peace, the helmet of salvation, and I take up the sword of the Spirit and the shield of faith.

As Connie said, "At first this prayer time was awkward. Over time it became normal. Now its awkward if we don't do it. If we miss a day, we usually can tell by about 3 o'clock in the afternoon. We'll look at each other and say, 'Oh! We didn't pray today.'"

How long does it take to pray through putting on the armor of God?

It can be less than twenty seconds per person.

This prayer is not meant to be a really long part of the day. Adding this should not require a major shift in your daily schedule.

But here is why this is so important.

When lions hunt, they don't take down the strongest of the herd.

They take down the weakest.

The accuser goes after the weakest member of the family. If you are seeking to glorify God in your life, the accuser focuses on the place he can gain the most leverage, the most advantage. Often this is the marriage. Often this is the children.

Or look at your own life. Where do you notice attacks the most? In your greatest gifting? That's strategic. In the area you already struggle? That's also strategic.

The enemy has a strategy against you. Do you have a strategy against him?

Resist the enemy's strategy in the authority Jesus gives you. "Submit yourselves, then, to God. Resist the devil, and he will flee from you."[4]

And if you want to try a longer biblical prayer of protection, see Appendix A.

THE PRACTICAL PRAYER OF PROTECTION

Heal the sick, raise the dead, cleanse those who have leprosy, drive out demons. Freely you have received; freely give.[5]

Every day, Bob and I pray a prayer of protection over ourselves and our community.

I am not the most patient person. I don't love repeating the same things over and over.

Early on, I silently protested to the Lord: *Surely I do not have to keep praying this prayer of protection every day.*

One day the Lord reminded me: Pray the prayer of protection.

And I protested, *No! I prayed it yesterday! That should be good for today, too!*

That evening, Bob hit a deer. Though he and his wife weren't hurt, their car needed repairs. Annoying and unpleasant.

When I heard about the accident, I said, *Lord, I repent! I repent! I will pray for protection every day.*

The issue was not so much to put pressure on me to perfectly execute prayer, but rather to remind me to be obedient. The Lord had prompted me to pray, and I had refused. (More on the idea of responsibility, coming up next.)

At that time, we prayed the prayer of protection from

Judith and Francis MacNutt's Christian Healing Ministries (CHM), below.

It includes the line, *We bind up the powers of earth, air, water, fire, the netherworld and the satanic forces of nature. We break any curses, hexes or spells sent against us and declare them null and void.*

The author explained: "'Earth, air, fire, and water' are unfamiliar categories to most of us, but these are the main elements of the world as the ancients divided them. The reason we put them in the prayer are simply the categories that Satanists use in casting curses. For instance, demons that inhabit the 'air' can cause hurricanes. You need not use these categories, of course, if you had rather not. We are simply breaking curses by reversing them in the same terms that Satanists use."[6]

Let me note: I didn't grow up in a family or culture where we would talk a whole lot about curses, hexes, and spells. If anything, these seemed like imaginary threats, about as realistic as an animated movie.

So I was surprised when I went through Francis MacNutt's *Deliverance* training. He said, "There are 63 active covens in Jacksonville, Florida."[7]

Covens, small groups of actively practicing witches, specifically target ministries and churches by name.

At the time he said that, Jacksonville was a city of perhaps a half million people.

Think of 63 regular gatherings seeking the downfall of the kingdom of God.

That's a lot of active resistance in a population.

If you attend church, or serve with a ministry, recognize that you have people who seek to be at enmity with you, who target you specifically.

And so we pray against their efforts. We serve the great God, and the great King above all gods.

Amen!

THE PRAYER OF PROTECTION[8]

In the name of Jesus Christ and by the power of his Cross and his Blood, we bind up the power of any evil spirits and command them not to block our prayers. We bind up the powers of earth, air, water, fire, the netherworld and the satanic forces of nature. We break any curses, hexes or spells sent against us and declare them null and void. We break the assignments of any spirits sent against us and send them to Jesus to deal with them as he will. Lord, we ask you to bless our enemies by sending your Holy Spirit to lead them to repentance and conversion. Furthermore, we bind all interaction and communication in the world of evil spirits as it affects us and our ministry. We ask for the protection of the shed blood of Jesus Christ over _____.

Thank you, Lord, for your protection and we ask that you send your angels to help us in the battle. We ask you to guide us in our prayers: share with us your Spirit's power and compassion. Amen.

OUR RESPONSIBILITY

Can any one of you by worrying add a single hour to your life?[9]

In 2009, my family moved to unimproved land in central Virginia, where everything was trying to kill us. Snakes, ticks, systemic poison ivy.

I had enough prayer background to know that I should pray a prayer of protection. I genuinely feared for our lives, so I dutifully prayed for protection every day.

But one day I wondered if maybe I was treating this prayer of protection like a mantra, something I prayed every day "just because." Was this some sort of magical thinking?

That day my husband was building a fence with T-posts. He took a 35-pound metal cylinder and slammed it into the top of a metal T-post. Brute strength to force metal into hard clay.

It's not rocket science; it's just hard work.

At one point, though, as he rammed down with all his strength, the cylinder caught on the edge of the post and rebounded into his forehead.

He called for me, and then screamed in a panic, as his hands were covered in blood. I ran outside to find my husband crumpled on the ground.

We compressed the head wound and the bleeding stopped. He was woozy for the rest of the day from a concussion.

No apparent permanent injury, so this could have been a lot worse. But it scared me.

I resumed praying the prayer of protection.

Some time later, my husband went to pick up an enormous stack of cattle panels. He had taken our four boys and was in the truck, driving home, when someone cut him off. With the load he was towing, the truck almost flipped.

When he told me this, I thought back through my morning and realized: I had forgotten to pray the prayer of protection.

I thought, "My family almost died today. I didn't pray the prayer of protection, and my family almost died."

And my follow-up to that was: *God, I'm not perfect. I'll never be perfect. I can't handle the pressure to be perfect lest my family will die. I'm out.*

And other than a little prayer here and there, I didn't pray much … for the next eight years.

I didn't want to be a target. I feared the enemy's reprisal. I knew I wouldn't pray perfectly and the idea that my imperfection could cause a family member's death terrified me.

I needed additional understanding—including a better understanding of the bounds of my responsibility.

Healing prayer minister Ken Polsley had a season in his life where he prayed every day at the cardiac ICU in his hometown. "Every one of those was a potentially terminal case. If I thought that it was my prayers that were going to restore any of those people, I couldn't have done it. That would have been far too much pressure."

We have the privilege to partner with God in what he's doing in the world, but the responsibility is, ultimately, his. As God directs, we can partner with him and shine the spotlight of God's grace on others. But God is the one at work.

God does not limit his protection based on our prayers.

We can pray for protection for ourselves and for others. But *how* God chooses to answer is up to him.

Looking back, I can see that my husband and sons weren't in an accident, despite my lack of prayer that day.

God protected them, that day, and every day.

———•✹•———

Lord, we agree with Paul when he said that you are before all things, and in you all things hold together.[10] *Thank you that you don't expect us to hold all things together. Great is your faithfulness. Amen.*

NEXT-LEVEL PROTECTION

Before they call I will answer; while they are still speaking I will hear.[11]

After a year and a half of praying the prayer of protection, I would finish the prayer and think, "I need more cleansing. I need more broken off."

Around this time, I was privileged to visit again with my college mentor Connie.

We swapped stories for hours.

She said, "Amy, for years, we would pray the Ephesians 6 armor of God, and we would pray the Psalm 91 protection, where God covers us with his feathers. We would pray the Christian Healing Ministries' prayer of protection. But we didn't have the breakthrough coverage that we needed. If anything, we felt exposed, not protected. We finally asked God, *What do we do? Lord, we are praying as best we know how, but we don't have coverage to the extent that we need.*"

Then she heard about a prayer by Mike Flynn, a man with a strong deliverance ministry out of California.

People would come to Jesus out of witchcraft, out of the demonic, out of the occult, and they would say, "We will teach you how to protect yourselves better against what we used to send against you to harm you. Then you will better be able to pray protection prayers against all that we used to bring against you."

In reading over Flynn's prayer for the first time, I was fascinated to see that, though I had been praying against curses, hexes, and spells, his prayer had all three of those, but 17 additional impingements, as well as healing of the body, soul, mind, and spirit.

Far more comprehensive.

Connie said, "When we found this prayer and started praying it, we began to have real breakthrough. The things that had been spiraling down actually shifted."

That afternoon, I went and prayed this with my sister. Jonelle is an involuntary seer, someone who can see into the spiritual realm. As we prayed, she said, "I see blackness coming off of us that we didn't know was on us."

In the months since I learned this prayer, I have prayed it and shared it with others. I have heard numerous testimonies of precious brothers and sisters, mighty people of prayer, who had been experiencing issues in themselves or their families—rebellion, mental illness, addiction, shaky income, illness—until they began to pray this prayer.

This prayer shifts things.

It is, indeed, a strong warfare prayer.

STRONG WARFARE PRAYER

I bind up the power of any evil spirits and command them not to block my prayers.[12]

I ask for the protection of the shed blood of Jesus Christ over _____.

Thank you, Lord, for your protection. I ask that you send angels to help me in the battle. I ask you to guide me in my prayers. Share with me your Spirit's power and compassion.

(The next four sentences are optional.)

I sign myself with the sign of the cross. (Do it.)

I cover myself with the Blood of the Lamb. (Some motion to convey covering.)

I surround myself with the Light of the Cross. (Circumscribe a circle around you.)

And in the Name of Jesus Christ, nothing shall come through to hurt me.

In the name of Jesus Christ crucified, died and risen, I bind all spirits of the air, the atmosphere, the water, the fire, the wind, the ground, the underground, and the nether world. I also bind the influence of any lost or fallen soul who may be present, and all emissaries of the satanic headquarters or any coven of witches or warlocks or Satan worshippers who may be present in some preternatural way. I claim the blood of Jesus on the air and atmosphere, the water, the fire, the wind, the ground and their fruits all around us, the underground and the nether world. Lord, I ask You to bless our enemies by sending your Holy Spirit to lead them to repentance and conversion.

In the name of Jesus Christ I forbid every adversary mentioned to communicate with or help one another in any way or to communicate with me, except as I permit.

In the name of Jesus Christ I seal this place and all present and all family and associates of those present and their places and possessions and sources of supply in the blood of Jesus.

(Repeat paragraph three times if you think someone has cursed you.)[13]

In the name of Jesus I forbid any lost spirits, covens, satanic groups or emissaries or any of their associates, subjects or superiors to harm or take revenge on me, my family, my associates, or cause harm or damage to anything we have.

In the name of Jesus Christ and by the merits of His precious blood, I break, decommission and dissolve every curse, hex, seal, spell, sorcery, bond, snare, trap, device, lie, stumbling block, obstacle, deception, diversion or distraction, spiritual chain or spiritual influence, every temptation, accusation or harassment, also every disease of body, soul, mind or spirit placed upon us, or on this place, or on any of the persons, places, and things mentioned, by any agent, or brought on us by our own mistakes or sins.

(Repeat this paragraph three times if under a curse.)
Amen.

ALWAYS PRAY AND DON'T GIVE UP

Then Jesus told his disciples a parable to show them that they should always pray and not give up.[14]

Connie and I compared notes on how long we might need to pray before we get a breakthrough.

Could we just pray this Strong Warfare Prayer one time, and have everything break off?

Not a simple answer.

Clearly, a single time is efficacious. My sister saw blackness leave us the first time we prayed.

So, yes, pray the Strong Warfare Prayer at least once.

But there's more to the story than that.

I think about how Jesus prayed, and how he taught his disciples to pray.

Jesus taught *daily* prayer.

Think about the Lord's Prayer: "This, then, is how you should pray: 'Our Father in heaven, hallowed be your name, your kingdom come, your will be done, on earth as it is in heaven. Give us today our daily bread. And forgive us our debts, as we also have forgiven our debtors. And lead us not into temptation, but deliver us from the evil one.'"[15]

Bob and I happily pray the Lord's Prayer every day.

Every day we hallow the name of the Lord. Every day we ask for his kingdom to come and his will to be done. Every day we ask for food, for forgiveness.

And every day we ask not to be led into temptation, but to be delivered from the evil one.

Delivered from the evil one.

Ideally, pray the prayer daily.

And recognize that some prayers take time to come to their fullness.

Early in my own experience of praying for businesses, I had gone to pray over a business and soon realized that I could not actually be on site for more than four hours. It was too intense spiritually for me.

Instead, for about four weeks, I walked and prayed in the neighborhood nearby, walking 20 miles or so per day, walking and praying. I prayed in English. I prayed in tongues. I cried. I worshipped.

I don't often get visions, but after four weeks, I had this picture of something like a black octopus over the building. And the Lord said, Today you get to cut off two legs.

So I pictured taking the sword of the Spirit in hand, and cut two legs off.

About a week later, the Lord said, Now it's time for the black octopus to go away.

I poked it with the sword, and, like an inflatable toy, all the air came out of it and it was nothing anymore.

But it had been an entity over that business.

I shared this with Connie and she said, "This is the way it is on college campuses, too. When we go in to start a new ministry, we will have the staff workers go walk and pray, maybe eight hours a day for a few months, before they're actually ready in the Spirit to take new ground."

When you first establish an enterprise, it takes focus and intentionality and extra prayer.

Which is to say: if you're in a season where you haven't

yet gotten the breakthrough, it's coming. Your prayers are not wasted.

"Be unceasing and persistent in prayer."[16]

May the Lord bless you as you keep praying.

———•✸•———

Lord, you teach us that we ought always to pray, and not give up. Give us strength to persist, and bless our prayers, Lord. Thank you! Amen!

CLEANSING

AFTER EVERY INTERACTION

After that, he poured water into a basin and began to wash his disciples' feet, drying them with the towel that was wrapped around him.[17]

Bob tells the story of his mentor Rosemarie Claussen. Her father was a high-ranking German military officer. The day she was born, her father went to work extra happy, and his superior officer asked why he was in such a good mood. "I have a daughter!"

"I'd like to be the godfather of your child."

That's how Rosemarie Claussen's birth certificate came to list the name of her godfather: Adolf Hitler.

She grew up with a deep sense of the importance of alliances.

Later, when Corrie ten Boom mentored Rosemarie, Corrie taught about the power of prayer to cut off alliances and connections.

We all need this teaching.

When we go through our day and interact with others, we form connections. As we interact with others, we can sometimes take on their problems.[18]

I usually pray the cutting-free prayer once a day. I also

pray it after every teaching call, after any travel (road trip, hotel stay, or plane), and usually at the end of a day of client interactions.

In addition, sometimes I think, "I started off today so cheerful and enthusiastic. What went wrong?"

And when I think back over the day, usually I will remember an interaction that left me under a gray cloud.

Then I pray the cutting-free prayer again.

Occasionally when I pray this one, I cry. In those cases, I pray it repeatedly until I don't cry any more. I assume that my tears are giving me insight into what my spirit needs.

THE CUTTING-FREE PRAYER

Lord Jesus, thank you for sharing with us your wonderful ministry of healing and deliverance. Thank you for the healings we have seen and experienced today. We realize that the sickness and evil we encounter is more than our humanity can bear, so cleanse us of any sadness, negativity or despair that we may have picked up. If our ministry has tempted us to anger, impatience or lust, cleanse us of those temptations and replace them with love, joy and peace. If any evil spirits have attached themselves to us or oppressed us in any way, we command you, spirits of earth, air, fire, water, the netherworld and the satanic forces of nature, to depart—now—and go straight to Jesus Christ for him to deal with you as he will.

Come Holy Spirit: renew us—fill us anew with your power, your life, your joy, and your wisdom. Strengthen us where we have felt weak and clothe us with your light. Fill us with life. Lord Jesus, please send your holy angels to minister to us and our families—guard us and protect us from all sickness, harm and accidents. We praise you now and forever, Father, Son and Holy Spirit, and we ask these things in Jesus' Holy Name that he may be glorified. Amen.[19]

FOR THE EMPATHETIC AMONG US

The spirits of prophets are subject to the control of prophets. For God is not a God of disorder but of peace—as in all the congregations of the Lord's people.[20]

My friend Emma is an empath. She said, "I literally soak up the negative emotions and atmosphere anywhere I go. I was asking God once how it is that one moment I am full of joy and then almost immediately can be in a dark, angry mood. All I did was walk into a new building or shake hands with someone new. Total strangers can set me off."

God said, You will need to learn with me how to manage and have boundaries so you don't soak it up. You can still understand and have discernment for people and situations—just don't take on what they carry.

And that is lovely, but, practically, how might one do this?

Once I went on an eagerly anticipated, long-delayed trip. Vibrating with happiness, I blithely set off, expecting a garden party.

Instead I found I was in a war zone.

And war zones aren't necessarily bad, if one is prepared, but I showed up in a sundress and had left my grenade launcher at home. The environment made me feel absolutely crazy.

I found myself in tears in the home of friends. Two days later, I was back again, desperately in need of triage.

My friend said, "As I was praying for you, I had a picture of an analog multimeter."

An analog multimeter is an electrical monitoring device, where the same dial can be adjusted to measure electricity multiple ways.

An electrician starts with the multimeter on the least sensitive scale, where it measures a range from 0 to 500. One degree is only 1/500th of the total.

Then the electrician can adjust it to 1/250th, or 1/100th, and even down to 1/10th, which is exquisitely sensitive. By that point, one degree is ten percent of the whole.

With an analog multimeter, you can *click-click* the dial and change the sensitivity.

Ideally, in any given situation, electricians want the reading to be in the middle of the multimeter: sensitive, but not blasted into oblivion.

My friend said, "I'm imparting to you the gift of the Holy Spirit, that you get to be an analog multimeter from now on. And you get to only sense the things that the Holy Spirit is sending you to sense. Start with the least sensitive, at that 1 to 500 scale. And if you're not picking up on anything, then *click-click* over to be more sensitive. But you don't need to be blown away."

We each get to be appropriately sensitive in any given environment.

A few weeks after this trip, I got an email where I thought, "This person is so depressed, I'm ready to kill myself.... *Oh! Let me be less sensitive!*" I had permission to *click-click* away from that deep sorrow. Then I could pray without the sense of drowning.

When the apostle Paul wrote, "The spirits of the prophets are subject to the control of the prophets,"[21] I interpret this to mean that we each get to control our responses to things.

You can find a few examples of this prayer in practice in Appendix B.

———•✸•———

I ask, Lord, that for any of your children who might feel oversensitive, who might feel like they don't have the layers of protection they need, that you would give them the analog multimeter upgrade, that they would be able to click-click to less sensitivity as needed.

Thank you, Lord, that you teach us all things, and give us all the tools we need.

PRAYER FOR A BURDEN BEARER

Surely he took up our pain and bore our suffering, yet we considered him punished by God, stricken by him, and afflicted.[22]

There came a day when I was so overburdened with cares that I felt like I could hardly breathe. I felt almost panicky in my own skin.

I called my friend Cindy McFaden, desperate for something. Did I need healing prayer? Deliverance? A listening ear?

I didn't know, but I needed relief!

Cindy has gone through and practiced a lot of healing prayer over the years, including training with Elijah House.

"Some people are burden bearers. You are one. But we need to follow the example of Jesus, who is the great burden bearer. Pray this prayer aloud."

I prayed the prayer below, and felt a lift in my spirit.

I don't pray it often, but when I feel weighed down with the intensity of the needs of others, when I feel burdened, then I pray this prayer.

If you carry the weight of the world, or fear the future what-ifs; if you struggle with anxiety, or simply need some relief, this is a lovely prayer to keep in mind.

THE PRAYER FOR A FRESH START

Lord Jesus, I thank you for being our burden bearer. Lord, today I want to start anew in my burden-bearing gift. I release to you the burdens that I have carried on behalf of others up to this day. Lord, redeem this gift in me and teach me to operate in it properly, so that I will not be overwhelmed and confused anymore. Lord, I want to use this gift to help others find the freedom, healing, and joy that is found in you. Teach me to be sensitive and to be able to feel in my spirit within my relationship with you, for that is where being a burden bearer is most effective—and powerful. Amen.

CONCLUSION

Do not be anxious about anything, but in every situation, by prayer and petition, with thanksgiving, present your requests to God. And the peace of God, which transcends all understanding, will guard your hearts and your minds in Christ Jesus.[23]

One of my friends asked about this scripture: "'No weapon forged against you will prevail, and you will refute every tongue that accuses you. This is the heritage of the servants of the LORD, and this is their vindication from me,' declares the LORD."[24]

"Doesn't God throw down the weapons formed against us so they don't prevail, and stop the accusing tongues? Doesn't this happen automatically? Why doesn't God's grace just cover us?"

Such good questions!

I think God offers us riches that we can either lay hold of ... or not.

Sort of like the scripture that opened this section: do not be anxious about anything. The peace of God guards our hearts and minds.

God offers riches to us: a worry-free life, where we present our requests to God and move forward in peace.

But many followers of Jesus still worry sometimes.

Just because God offers us a gift doesn't mean that

we take it.

Perhaps some of God's promises come as optional gifts: we can either receive or not, as we choose.

But if we don't know we have a choice, how would we ever choose to receive?

"This day I call the heavens and the earth as witnesses against you that I have set before you life and death, blessings and curses. Now choose life, so that you and your children may live and that you may love the Lord your God, listen to his voice, and hold fast to him. For the Lord is your life, and he will give you many years in the land he swore to give to your fathers, Abraham, Isaac and Jacob."[25]

BLESSING

    And that about wraps it up. God is strong, and he wants you strong. So take everything the Master has set out for you, well-made weapons of the best materials. And put them to use so you will be able to stand up to everything the Devil throws your way. This is no weekend war that we'll walk away from and forget about in a couple of hours. This is for keeps, a life-or-death fight to the finish against the Devil and all his angels.
    Be prepared. You're up against far more than you can handle on your own. Take all the help you can get, every weapon God has issued, so that when it's all over but the shouting you'll still be on your feet. Truth, righteousness, peace, faith, and salvation are more than words. Learn how to apply them. You'll need them throughout your life. God's Word is an indispensable weapon. In the same way, prayer is essential in this ongoing warfare. Pray hard and long. Pray for your brothers and sisters. Keep your eyes open. Keep each other's spirits up so that no one falls behind or drops out.[26]

    I have seasons where I'm struck again and again with how much sadness and pain people carry. Broken marriages, broken work environments, broken relationships, broken health, broken systems, broken lives, broken dreams.

Do you sometimes find it hard to keep your head above water? No shame there.

"You're up against far more than you can handle on your own."

And yet, despite the direness of Paul's statement ... the end result is triumph.

God gives us help. We have a chance to stand on our feet.

"God is strong, and he wants you strong.... Pray hard and long. Pray for your brothers and sisters. Keep your eyes open. Keep each other's spirits up so that no one falls behind or drops out."

Thank you, Jesus, that you don't ask us to handle things on our own. You give us yourself and you give us the body of Christ, so that we won't be alone. And you give us weapons so that we have a fighting chance to still be on our feet. Thank you, Lord.

The Lord bless you as you seek his face.

APPENDIX

APPENDIX A
Pray Psalm 91

One of the most beautiful Psalms, Psalm 91, offers many promises.

You can simply read through, agreeing with the scripture. That might be as easy as literally reading, and as you read, assenting to the truth.

Or it might be a prayer of response.

Lord, your word says, "Whoever dwells in the shelter of the Most High will rest in the shadow of the Almighty." Lord, let me and my husband and my children dwell in that shelter. Give us the rest in your shadow that you promise.

Or you can personalize this Psalm for yourself and your loved ones.

Phil and Amy, Jadon, Isaiah, Abraham, Jonadab, and Caleb dwell in the shelter of the Most High. We rest in the shadow of the Almighty.

And so on, all the way through.

And be honest as you pray. If you aren't sure you agree with something, talk to God about it.

For example, this Psalm ends, *"He will call on me, and I will answer him; I will be with him in trouble, I will deliver him and honor him. With long life I will satisfy him and show him my salvation."*

Some years ago, when one of my dearest friends died at age 56, I was listening to the Sons of Korah sing a gorgeous version of this Psalm, and weeping at the end because it didn't feel true. Fifty-six years is not a long life!

And then they sang, "With a long, long, eternal life."

Ah. Yes.

Psalm 91

Whoever dwells in the shelter of the Most High will rest in the shadow of the Almighty.

I will say of the Lord, "He is my refuge and my fortress, my God, in whom I trust."

Surely he will save you from the fowler's snare and from the deadly pestilence.

He will cover you with his feathers, and under his wings you will find refuge; his faithfulness will be your shield and rampart.

You will not fear the terror of night, nor the arrow that flies by day,

nor the pestilence that stalks in the darkness, nor the plague that destroys at midday.

A thousand may fall at your side, ten thousand at your right hand, but it will not come near you.

You will only observe with your eyes and see the punishment of the wicked.

If you say, "The Lord is my refuge," and you make the Most High your dwelling,

no harm will overtake you, no disaster will come near your tent.

For he will command his angels concerning you to guard you in all your ways;

they will lift you up in their hands, so that you will not strike your foot against a stone.

You will tread on the lion and the cobra; you will trample the great lion and the serpent.

"Because he loves me," says the Lord, "I will rescue him; I will

*protect him, for he acknowledges my name.
He will call on me, and I will answer him; I will be with him in trouble, I will deliver him and honor him.
With long life I will satisfy him and show him my salvation."*

APPENDIX B
Examples of the Analog Multimeter Prayer

Grace and peace be yours in abundance through the knowledge of God and of Jesus our Lord. His divine power has given us everything we need for a godly life through our knowledge of him who called us by his own glory and goodness. Through these he has given us his very great and precious promises, so that through them you may participate in the divine nature, having escaped the corruption in the world caused by evil desires.[27]

A friend asked for some examples of the analog multimeter prayer.

Once I went to the state of Washington, where I prayed in various places and environments. At times, I needed more sensitivity, and at times I needed less.

- I stayed in a home of peace and joy. At one point, I walked through their home, and said, *Lord, if there's anything you want me to pay attention to, let me pray for that.*

  And nothing came to mind. It was a peaceful home of beauty. Even though I tried to make myself more sensitive, there wasn't much to sense.

- I visited a ministry location, a house near a public high school.

  There the sadness instantly brought me to tears.

  Was the sadness radiating from the school?

  Was it because the property used to be the gathering spot for the smokers and slackers, those who carry rejec-

tion and rebellion and anger and self-destruction?
Was it because the ministry itself was both seeking to take new ground and also sustaining hits?
Was it the sorrow of the leadership?
Or because the students who assembled came with both faithfulness and also their own angst?
Perhaps all of these and more.
In retrospect, the despair was so strong, I didn't need more sensitivity. I could probably have tried to be less so.

- I went to pray over a small business. There I intentionally tried to be more sensitive. One room felt off: the occupant was intentionally turning from God. Two rooms gave me headaches.
  But overall, it was a cheerful place of energy and hope ... exactly what I would expect from a building that had been prayed over and fought for in the spirit during many years.

- Another time I was out driving with my friends, going to pray over a new purchase they had made.
  We were talking happily, when suddenly, I thought, "Oh, I'm exhausted. I wish I could take a nap right now."
  We had just passed the city limits into a different town, one known in the area for its drug use.
  A place of lethargy and laziness and a desire to numb, a place of exhaustion and despair.
  I prayed for the believers in that town to be released to greater effectiveness, and that we would not be bound by a spirit of lethargy.
  But then I also realized that I didn't need to be so sensitive as I drove through this place. So I made myself less sensitive, as I didn't want to be so inundated with the feelings of that place.

Overall, as I went through my days in Washington, I was

APPENDIX

able to stay in a place of joy and hope and eager expectation, adjusting how sensitive I was at any given moment.

Thank you, Lord, that you do give us everything we need for a godly life through our knowledge of you who has called us. Teach us your way, Lord! Thank you! Amen!

NOTES

1. Ephesians 6:10-12
2. I Peter 5:8, emphasis mine
3. Ephesians 6:10-17
4. James 4:7
5. Matthew 10:8
6. https://www.christianhealingmin.org/images/CHM/downloads/PrayerforProtection2.pdf
7. A coven is a group of witches who meet regularly, a sort of anti-church, if you will.
8. https://www.christianhealingmin.org/images/CHM/downloads/PrayerforProtection2.pdf
9. Matthew 6:27
10. Colossians 1:17
11. Isaiah 65:24
12. This comes primarily from Mike Flynn's ministry. Others added their parts, and I added a bit from Christian Healing Ministries' prayer, too. You can find the original at https://www.freshwindministries.org/gifts/protection-prayers.html
    When praying this prayer with another person, or in a group, of course, change the "I" and "me" to "our" and "we."
13. In the paragraphs that recommend praying it three times, I suggest you do that not only the first time, but until you feel the Lord release you to stop. And even then, you might keep going. At one point, I thought, "I've prayed this daily for months; surely I have no more curses on me now!" And within four days I thought, "Why am I so tired? OH!" And I started repeating three times again, and immediately felt better. That might be unique to me, in the line of work I do, or it might be more universal.
14. Luke 18:1
15. Matthew 6:9-13
16. I Thessalonians 5:17 (AMP)
17. John 13:5
18. Some of that is, presumably, good. Scripture tells us in Galatians 6:2 to bear one another's burdens. But I think we're supposed to bear those burdens *to Jesus*, not carry them ourselves.
19. https://www.christianhealingmin.org/images/CHM/downloads/CuttingFreePrayer.pdf.
20. I Corinthians 14:32-33
21. I Corinthians 14:32
22. Isaiah 53:4
23. Philippians 4:6-7
24. Isaiah 54:17
25. Deuteronomy 30:19-20
26. Ephesians 6:10-18, *The Message*
27. II Peter 1:2-4

KEEP THESE PRAYERS ON YOUR PHONE

I keep these four prayers as separate notes on my phone. In some settings, I want the more simple "Prayer of Protection."

I pray the "Strong Warfare Prayer" and the "Cutting-Free Prayer" daily.

I pray the "Prayer for a Fresh Start" as needed.

To get the digital version of each of these, email amy@workplaceprayer.com.

ABOUT THE AUTHORS

Bob Perry has been a passionate student of prayer for more than four decades, constantly asking, "Lord, teach me to pray." He has founded and led multiple prayer initiatives that have trained and mobilized hundreds of thousands of people in prayer partnerships.

A.J. Lykosh loves healing and deliverance. Her heart's cry comes from the verse, "My people are destroyed for lack of knowledge" (Hosea 4:6). The author of several highly acclaimed books, she seeks to stop the destruction as best she can through writing and speaking. She sends daily emails about prayer, and podcasts at Make Prayer Beautiful.

Together, they run Workplace Prayer, to cover businesses in prayer, and Prayer Mentoring, to raise up healthy intercessors to bring the kingdom of God to bear in their lives and communities.

They love feedback. Email amy@workplaceprayer.com to start a conversation.

MAKARIOS PRESS

Be in your happy place.

AS IT IS IN HEAVEN
Why Workplace Prayer Exists

When Jesus taught on prayer, he began, "Our Father in heaven, hallowed be your name, your kingdom come, your will be done, on earth as it is in heaven." How can we effectively pray God's kingdom on earth, if we don't know what heaven looks like? If we want to pray better, we need to understand what we're praying for. Catch a glimpse of heaven in these short free verse poems, taken from Revelation 4 and 5. Pressed for time? You could read a single chapter. Or even a single poem!

> "I just sat down with your book. I am on the second page. In tears. Thank you. Beautiful and song-like. And fun." — **Sarah**

> "I feel like each line of each poem is like a choice morsel of truth that I just want to savor slowly. I set aside your book to read in quiet and cozy moments wrapped in a quilt on my bed. It is something I look forward to and cherish." — **Elena**

> "I love the short meditative chapters. It's great bedtime reading. Congratulations!!" — **Perry Marshall**

FIND OUT MORE AT
makariospress.com/heaven

THE PRINCE PROTECTS HIS CITY
Nehemiah Prayed Four Months, Then Rebuilt the Wall in Only 52 Days

A free verse look at the book of Nehemiah. Come meet a man who brought God's kingdom to bear in his work. Nehemiah wasn't a warrior or a king. He was a tremendous administrator, a gifted leader, a world-class historian, a treasured friend, a successful fund-raiser, and a prince. And he prayed constantly.

> "Loved it. Such a nice quick pace to read Nehemiah and also space to sit in parts if I just wanted to read one page" — **Angela**

FIND OUT MORE AT
amazon.com

ONE VOICE: THE STORY OF WILLIAM WILBERFORCE
Gorgeous Story of Tenacity + Courage

Biography in verse of the man who, despite all obstacles, fought to end the Slave Trade in Great Britain. Powerful story of tenacity and courage.

> "One Voice has become one of my absolute favourite books of all time. I was so skeptical when I realized it was written in free verse but oh, it's so, so special. I can't make it through without sobbing." — **Emily**

FIND OUT MORE AT
sonlight.com

21 DAYS OF A F(E)AST
A Fast That Feels More Like a Feast

Why fasting is a joy, and why you should do it. A guide for a fast that anyone can do, even if you can't restrict calories. The four types of fasting, and how to choose. Morning and evening readings for 21 days. Stories and testimonies. Drawn from four decades of experience and wisdom. Come sit in the Lord's presence.

> "Appreciating the wealth within this book!! Such a brilliant resource!" — **Nicole**

FIND OUT MORE AT
amazon.com

PRAYER REFRESH
Short Prayers to Pray Through Your Day

You don't have to completely change your life, your habits, your personality, or your social media usage in order to have a good prayer life. This book introduces a wide variety of prayers that you can pray in a minute or less, that will fit into your day, right where you are. Use it as a 21 day devotional, or read straight through.

> "The Prayer Refresh was so life changing, perspective shattering, and breathed so much, much needed life into me and our home that I long to go through it again. Regularly. Like monthly." — **Amanda**

FIND OUT MORE AT
amazon.com

JUNETEENTH: AN INVITATION TO FAST
Both the Why and the How To

Join us in a one-day fast. In Christ alone do we find peace, forgiveness, reconciliation, and restoration. Because we want more of these, we offer an invitation to fast on Juneteenth.

> "The booklet was so helpful with the historical summary of the date (which I knew nothing about), as well as specific prayers and family examples, to guide my focused petitions. The format is beautiful, and so clearly organized! Great resource!" — **Eileen**

FIND OUT MORE AT
amazon.com

GROW WITH PRAYER EXPERIENCES

Throughout the year, we offer a wide range of prayer experiences: Communal Fasts, Prayer Challenges, and Sacred Assemblies.

If you want to grow in prayer in creative and unexpected ways, come join us.

FIND OUT MORE AT
PrayerExperiences.com

Made in the USA
Columbia, SC
10 November 2022

70695339R00046